Summer Season Color By Number Book

This Color by Number Book belongs to:

———————————————

Copyright © 2020 Adult Puzzle Books

1. Black
2. Blue
3. Light Blue
4. Brown
5. Dark Red
6. Orange
7. Yellow
8. Purple
9. Pink
10. Gold
11. Green
12. Gold
13. Red
14. Dark Green

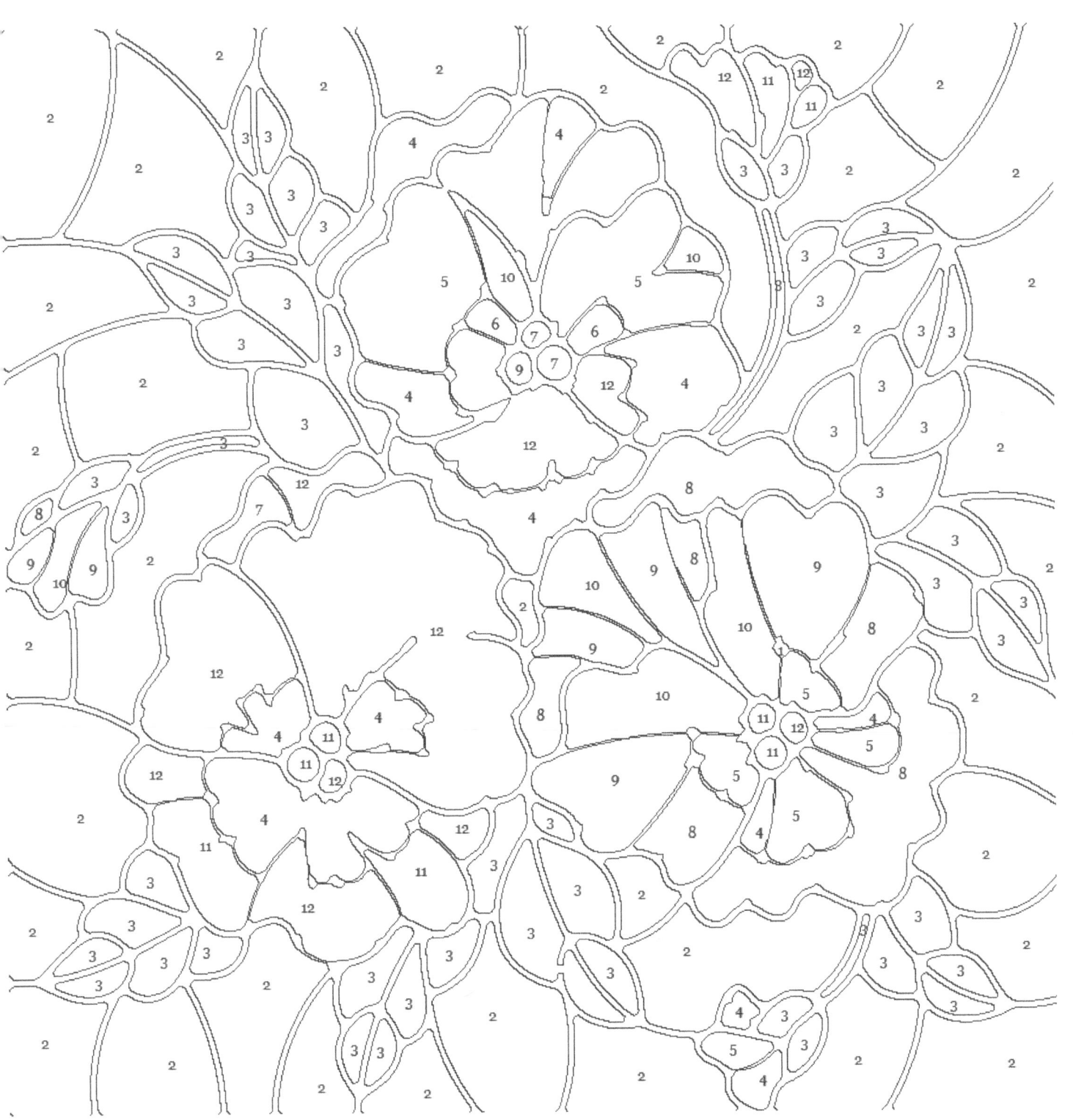

1. Black
2. Blue
3. Light Blue
4. Brown
5. Dark Red
6. Orange
7. Yellow
8. Purple
9. Pink
10. Gold
11. Green
12. Gold
13. Red
14. Dark Green

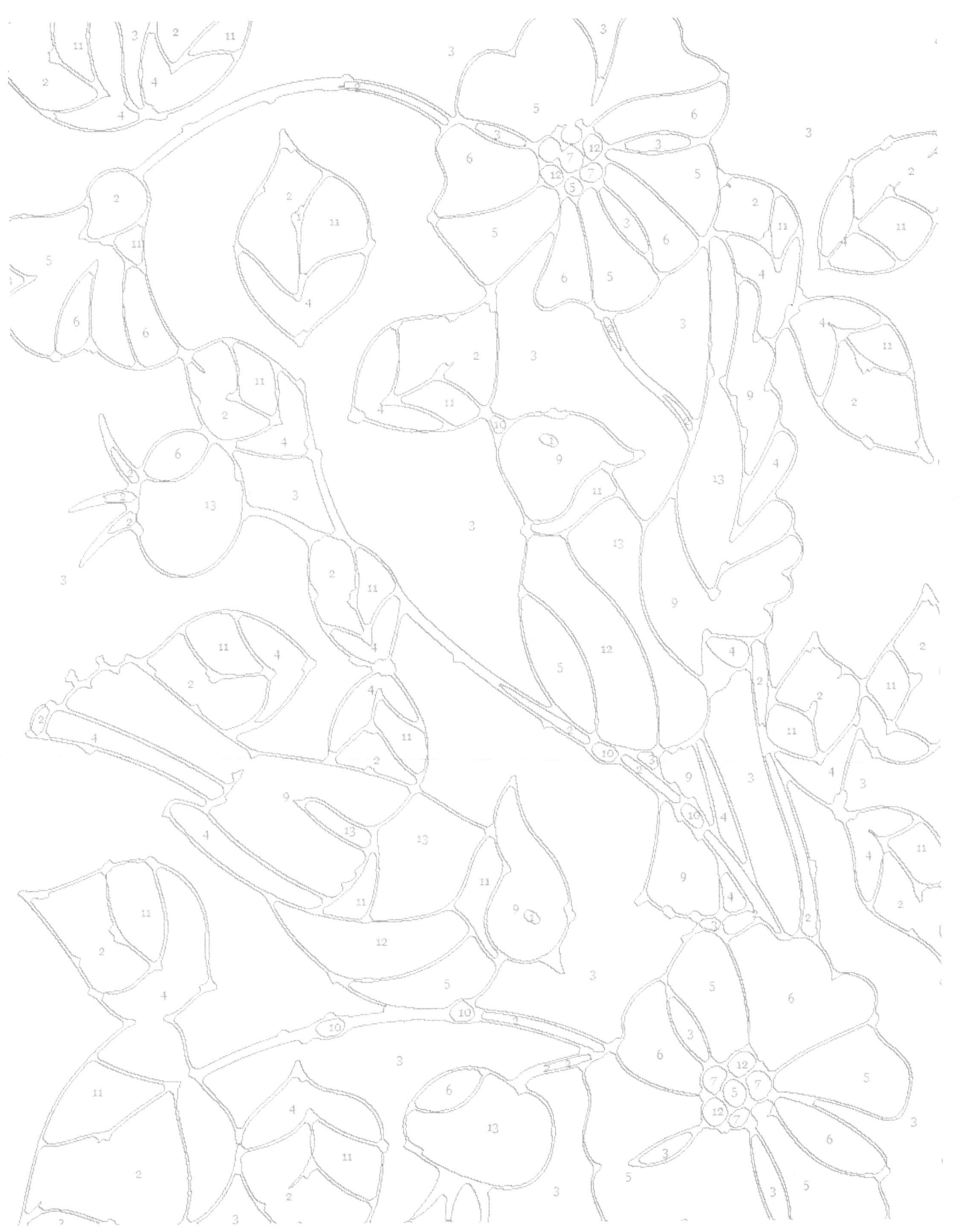

1. Black
2. Blue
3. Light Blue
4. Brown
5. Dark Red
6. Orange
7. Yellow
8. Purple
9. Pink
10. Gold
11. Green
12. Gold
13. Red
14. Dark Green

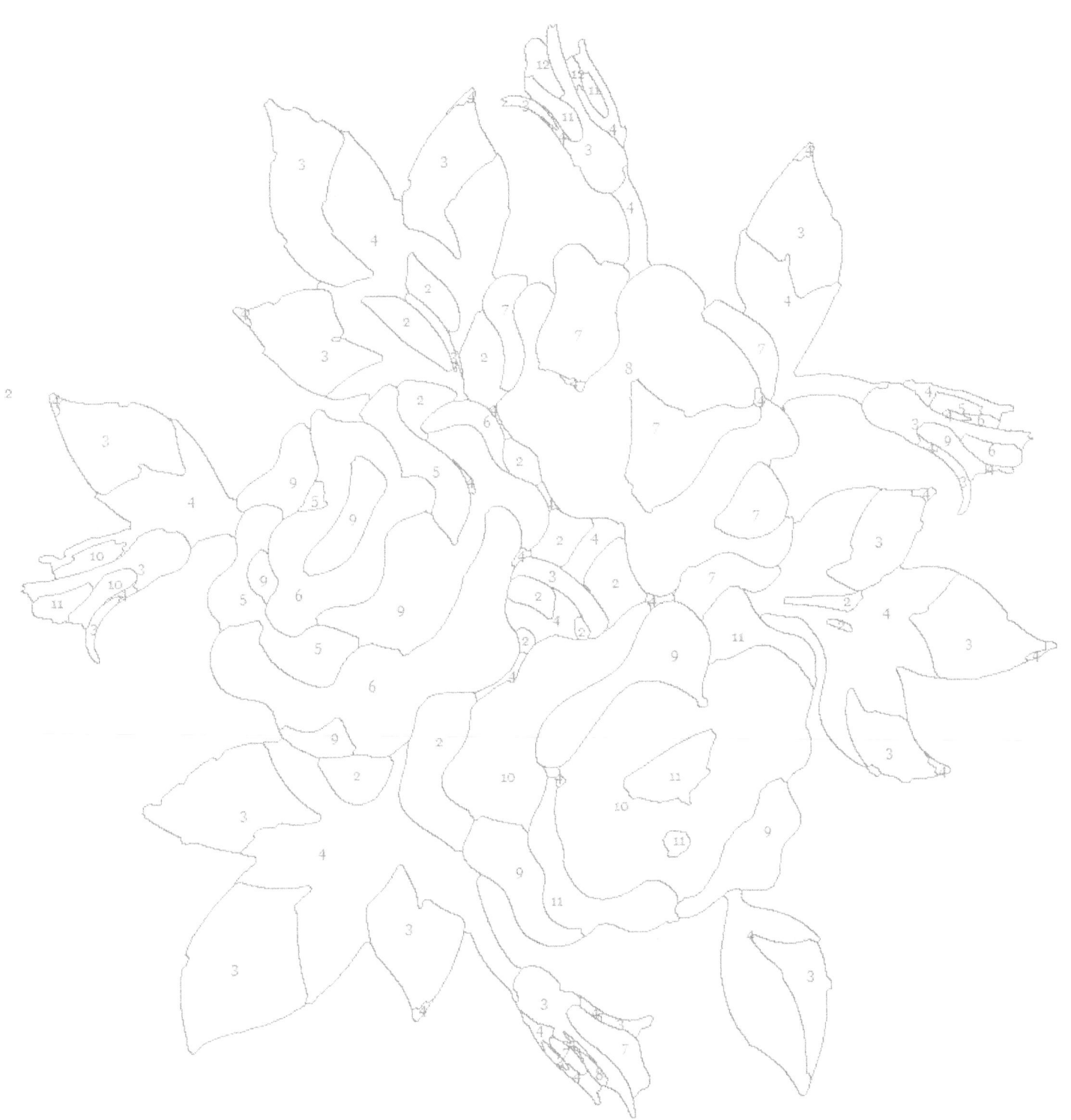

1. Black
2. Blue
3. Light Blue
4. Brown
5. Dark Red
6. Orange
7. Yellow
8. Purple
9. Pink
10. Gold
11. Green
12. Gold
13. Red
14. Dark Green

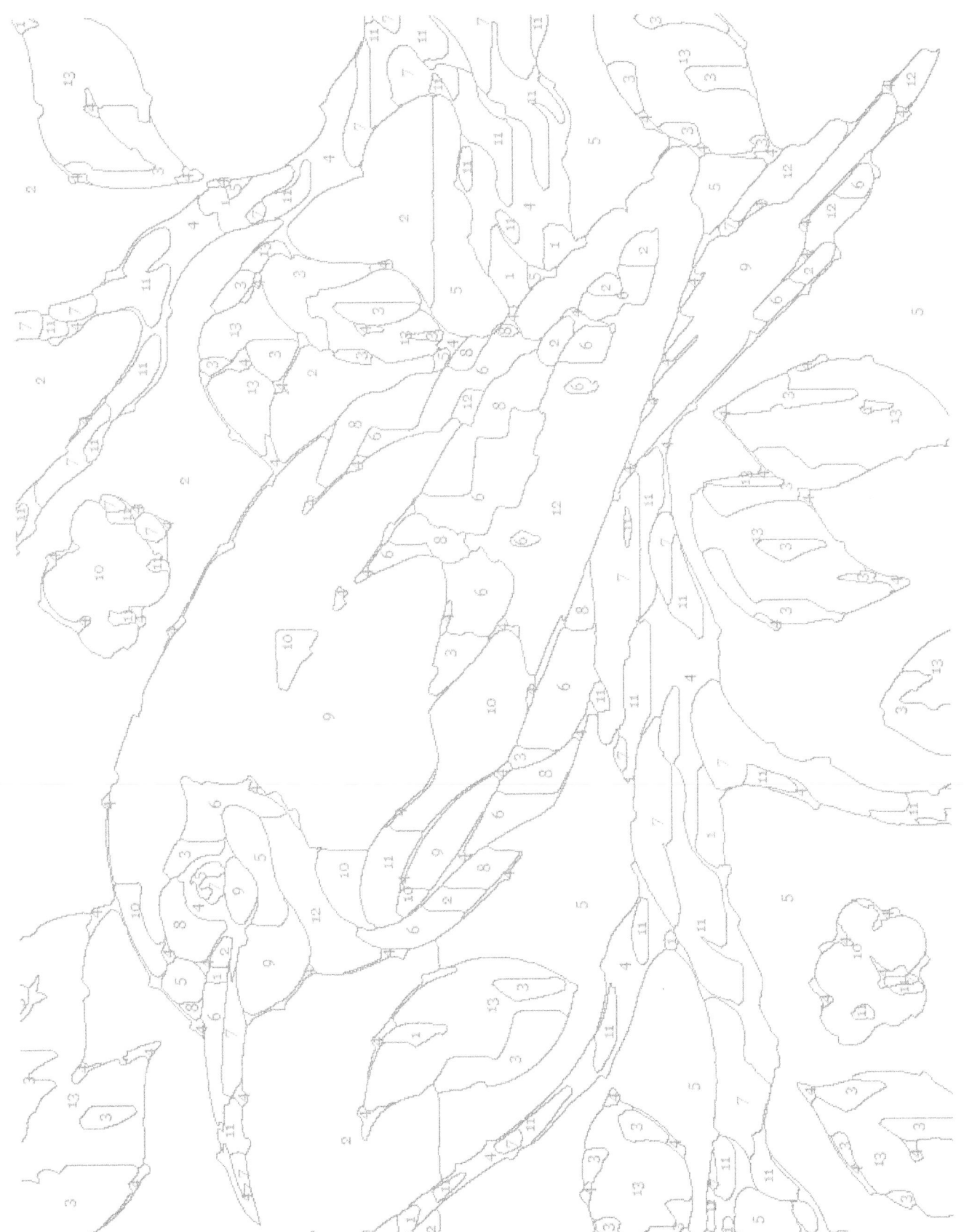

1. Black
2. Blue
3. Light Blue
4. Brown
5. Dark Red
6. Orange
7. Yellow
8. Purple
9. Pink
10. Gold
11. Green
12. Gold
13. Red
14. Dark Green

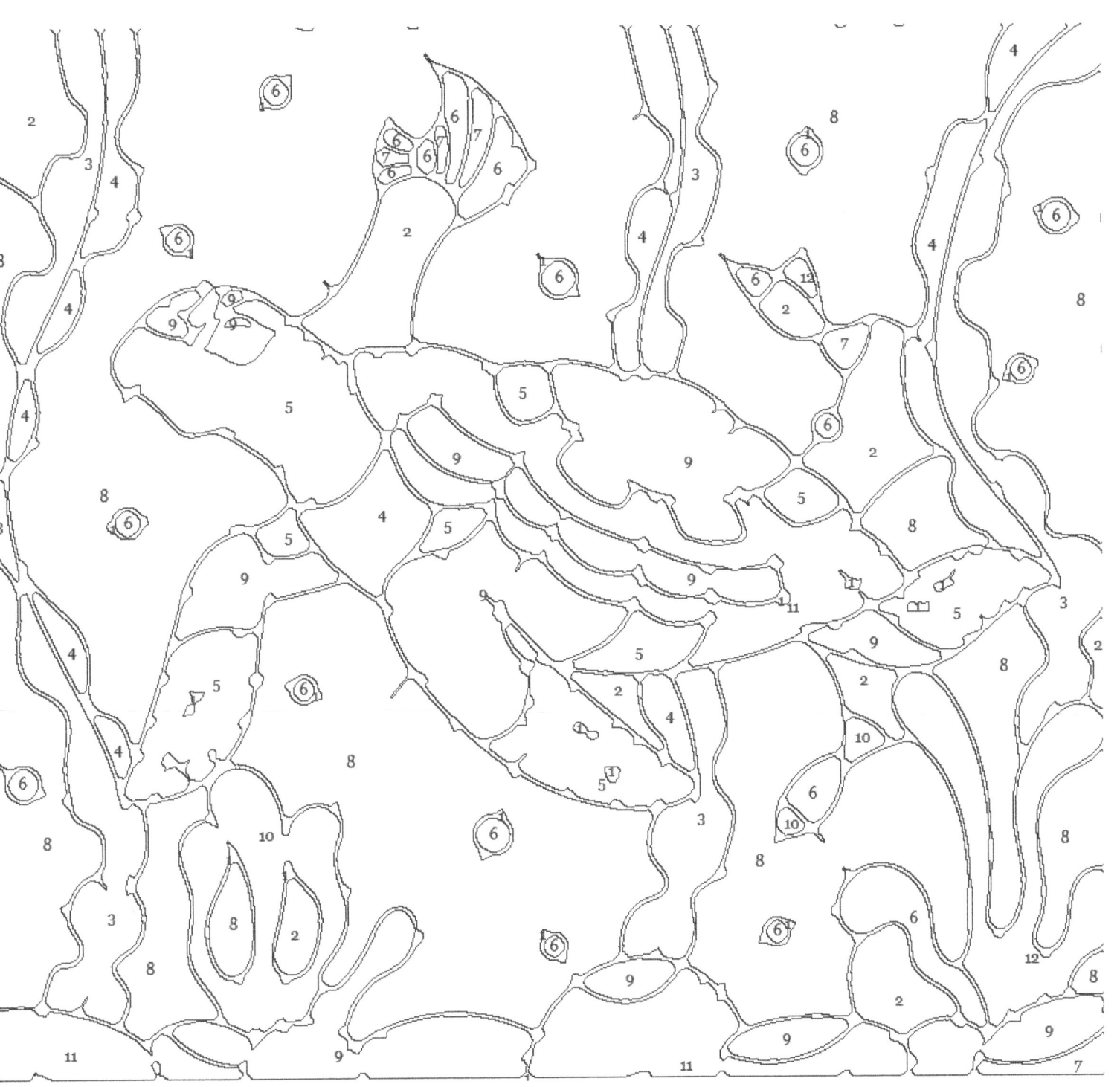

15. Black
16. Blue
17. Light Blue
18. Brown
19. Dark Red
20. Orange
21. Yellow
22. Purple
23. Pink
24. Gold
25. Green
26. Gold
27. Red
28. Dark Green

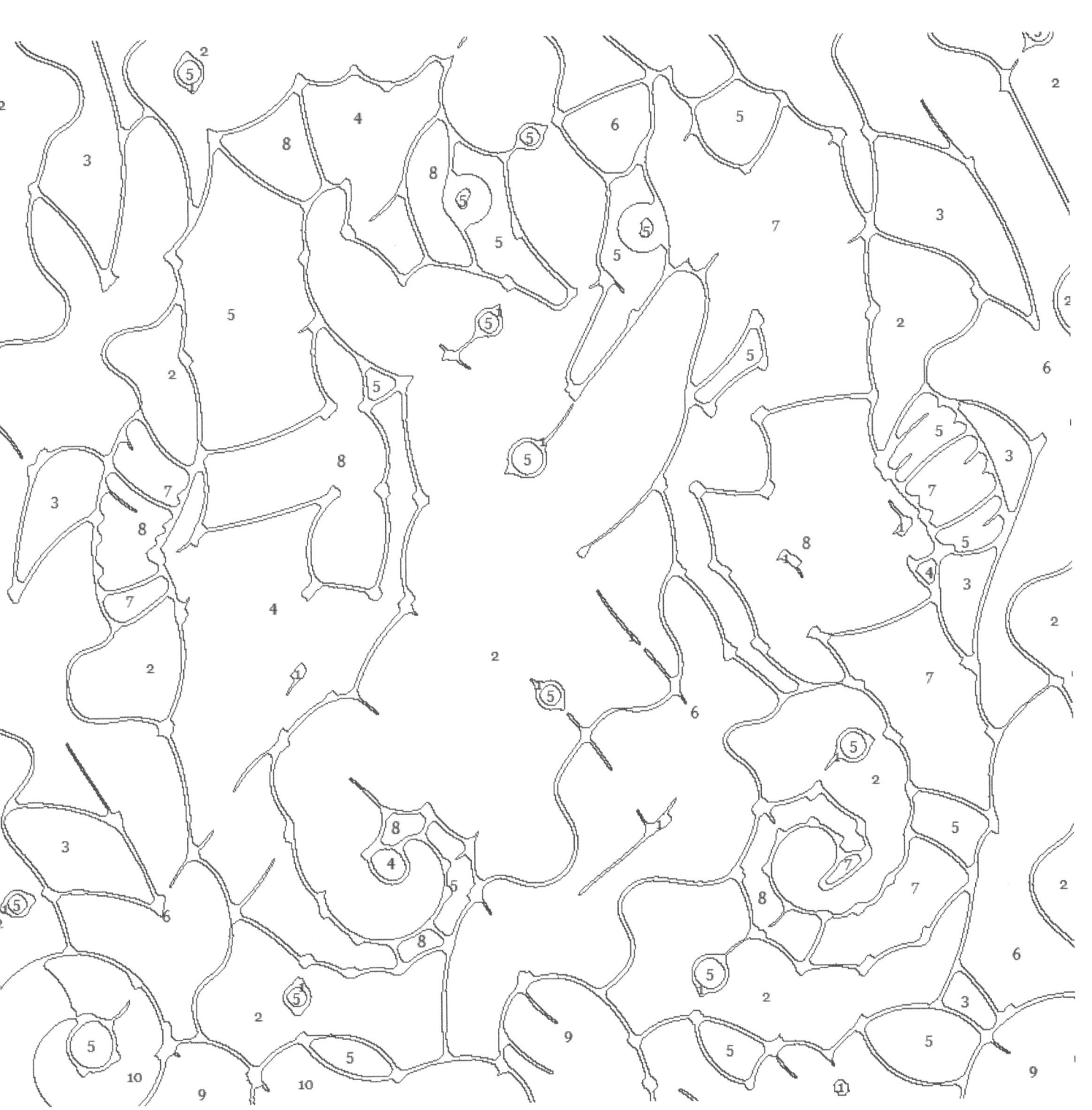

1. Black
2. Blue
3. Light Blue
4. Brown
5. Dark Red
6. Orange
7. Yellow
8. Purple
9. Pink
10. Gold
11. Green
12. Gold
13. Red
14. Dark Green

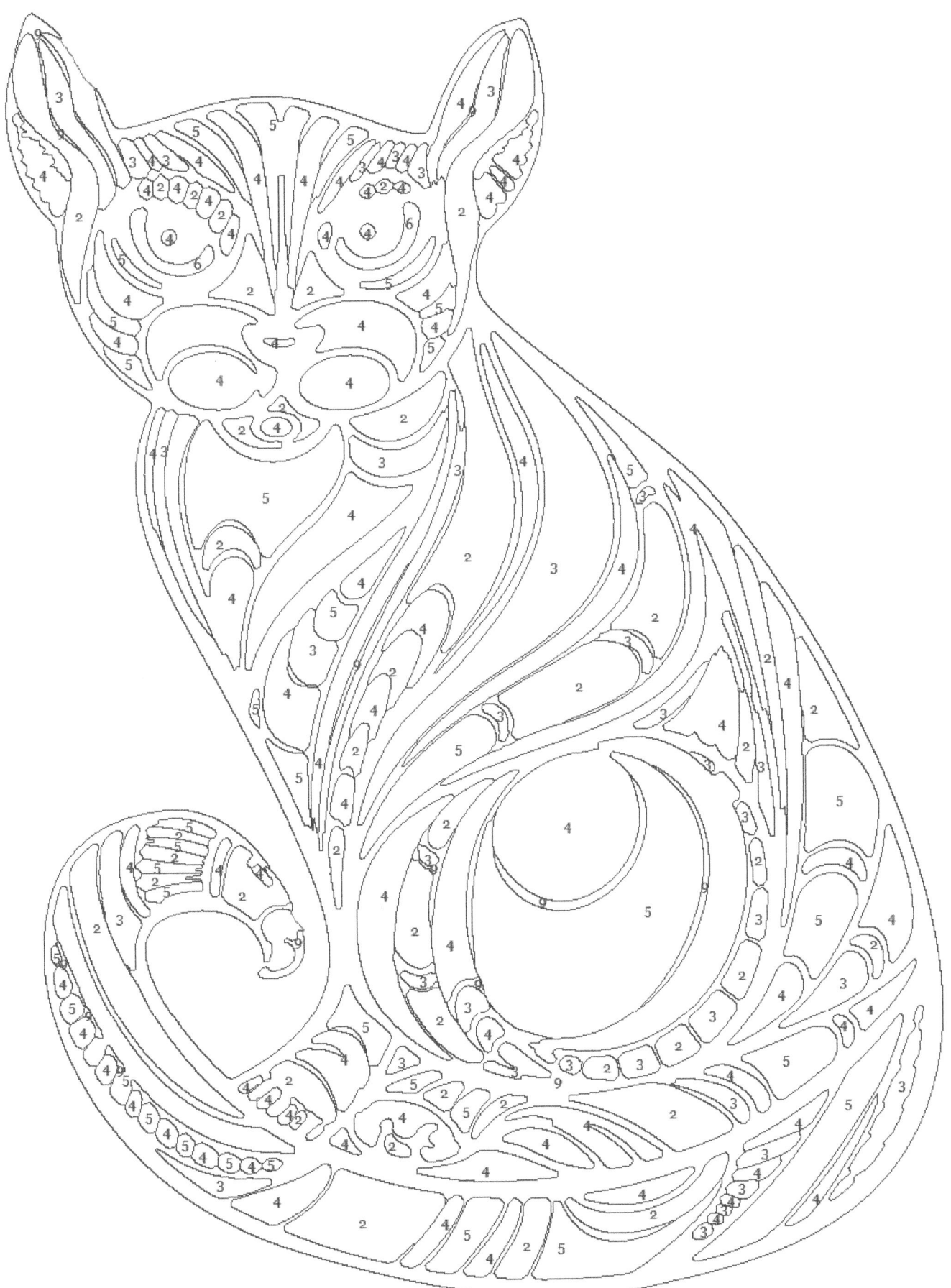

1. Black
2. Blue
3. Light Blue
4. Brown
5. Dark Red
6. Orange
7. Yellow
8. Purple
9. Pink
10. Gold
11. Green
12. Gold
13. Red
14. Dark Green

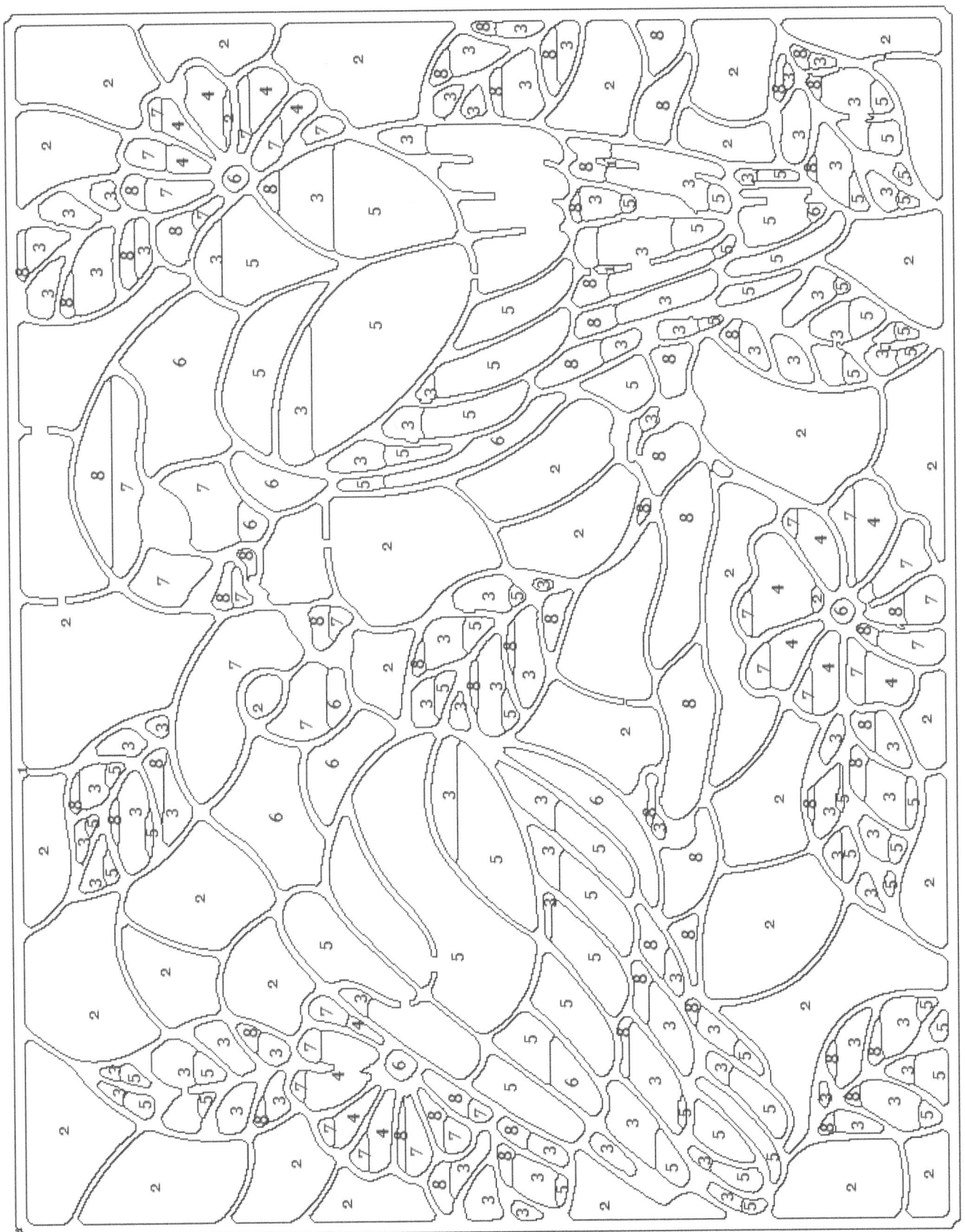

1. Black
2. Blue
3. Light Blue
4. Brown
5. Dark Red
6. Orange
7. Yellow
8. Purple
9. Pink
10. Gold
11. Green
12. Gold
13. Red
14. Dark Green

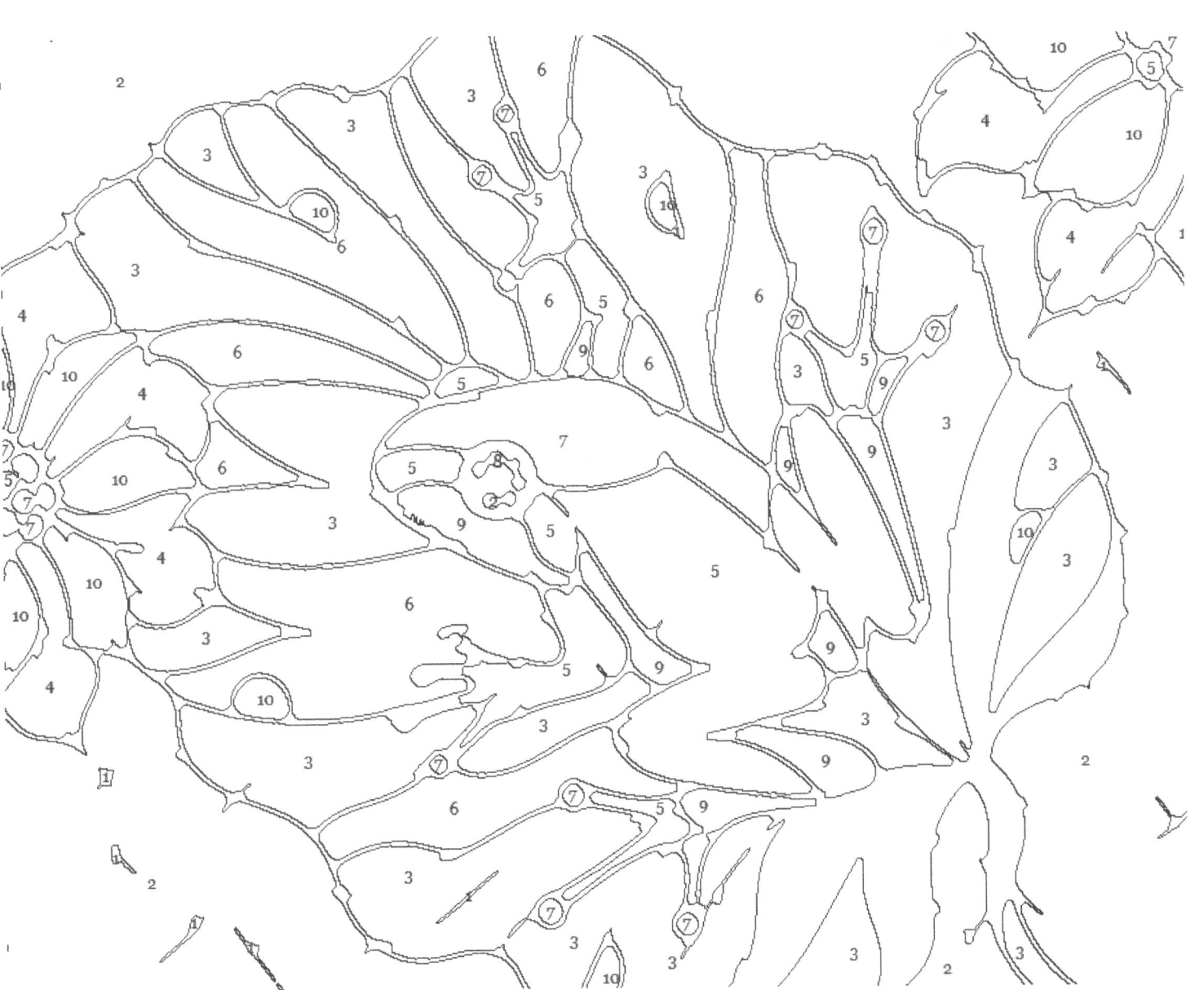

1. Black
2. Blue
3. Light Blue
4. Brown
5. Dark Red
6. Orange
7. Yellow
8. Purple
9. Pink
10. Gold
11. Green
12. Gold
13. Red
14. Dark Green

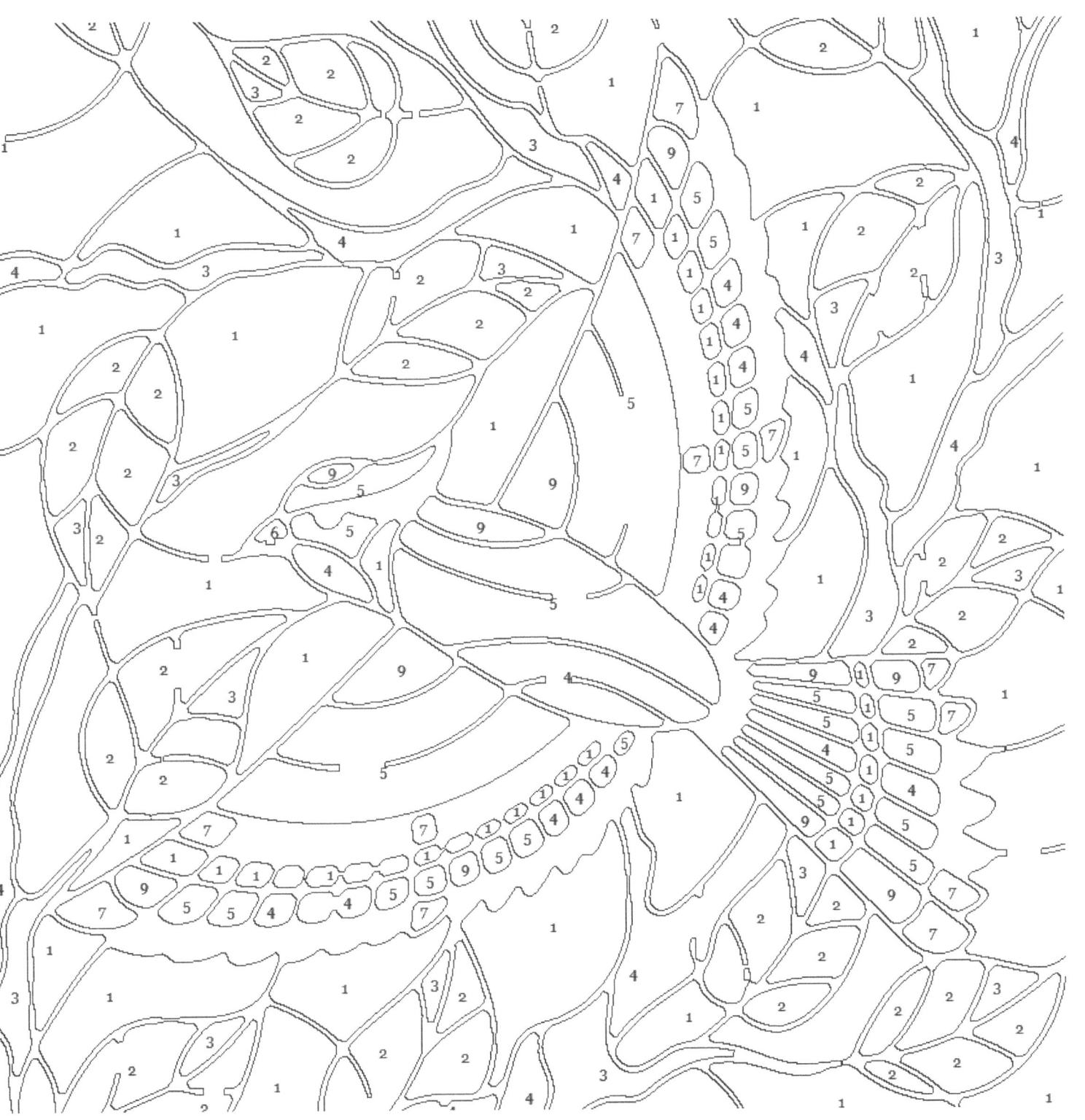

1. Black
2. Blue
3. Light Blue
4. Brown
5. Dark Red
6. Orange
7. Yellow
8. Purple
9. Pink
10. Gold
11. Green
12. Gold
13. Red
14. Dark Green

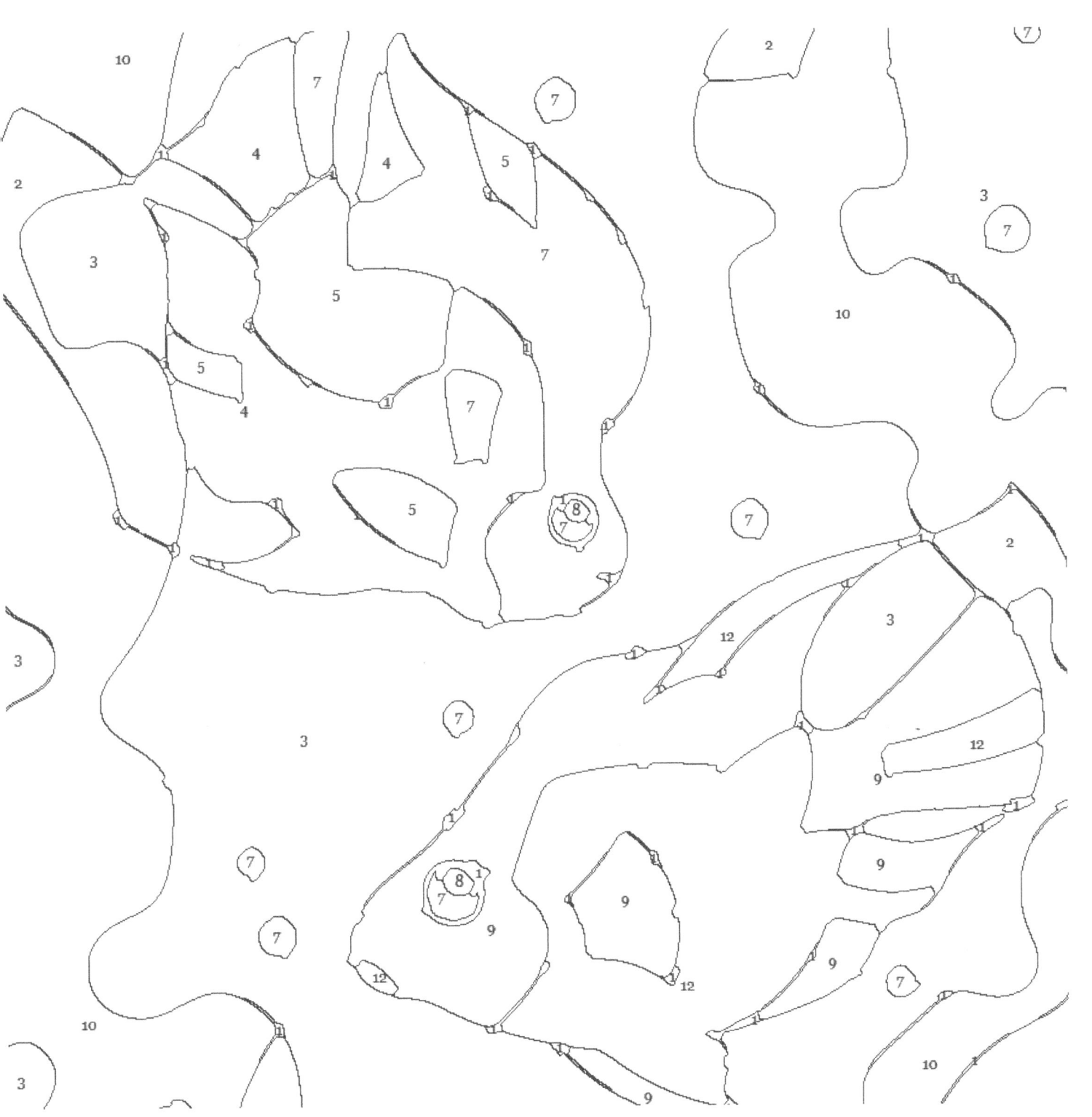

1. Black
2. Blue
3. Light Blue
4. Brown
5. Dark Red
6. Orange
7. Yellow
8. Purple
9. Pink
10. Gold
11. Green
12. Gold
13. Red
14. Dark Green

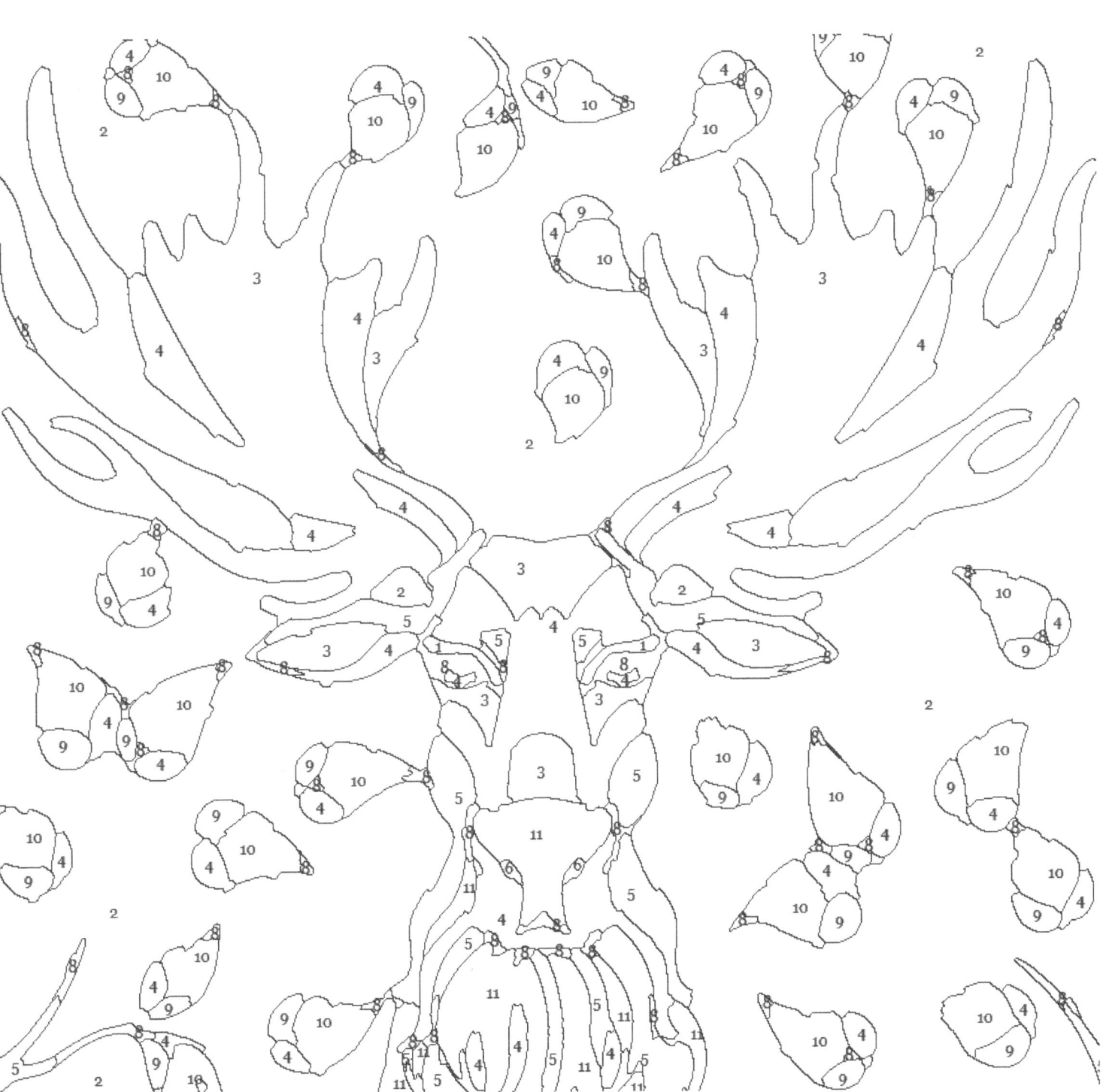

1. Black
2. Blue
3. Light Blue
4. Brown
5. Dark Red
6. Orange
7. Yellow
8. Purple
9. Pink
10. Gold
11. Green
12. Gold
13. Red
14. Dark Green

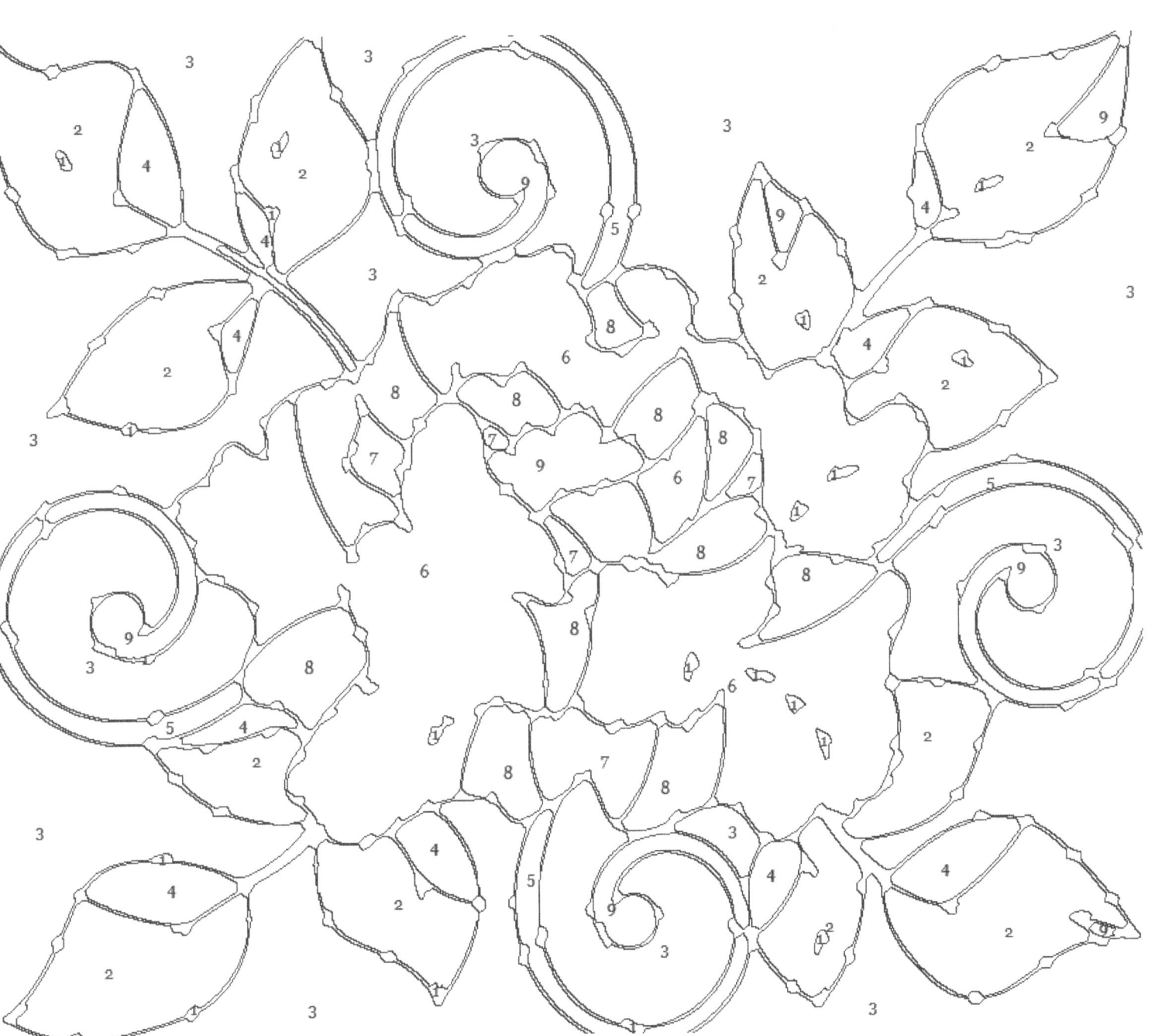

1. Black
2. Blue
3. Light Blue
4. Brown
5. Dark Red
6. Orange
7. Yellow
8. Purple
9. Pink
10. Gold
11. Green
12. Gold
13. Red
14. Dark Green

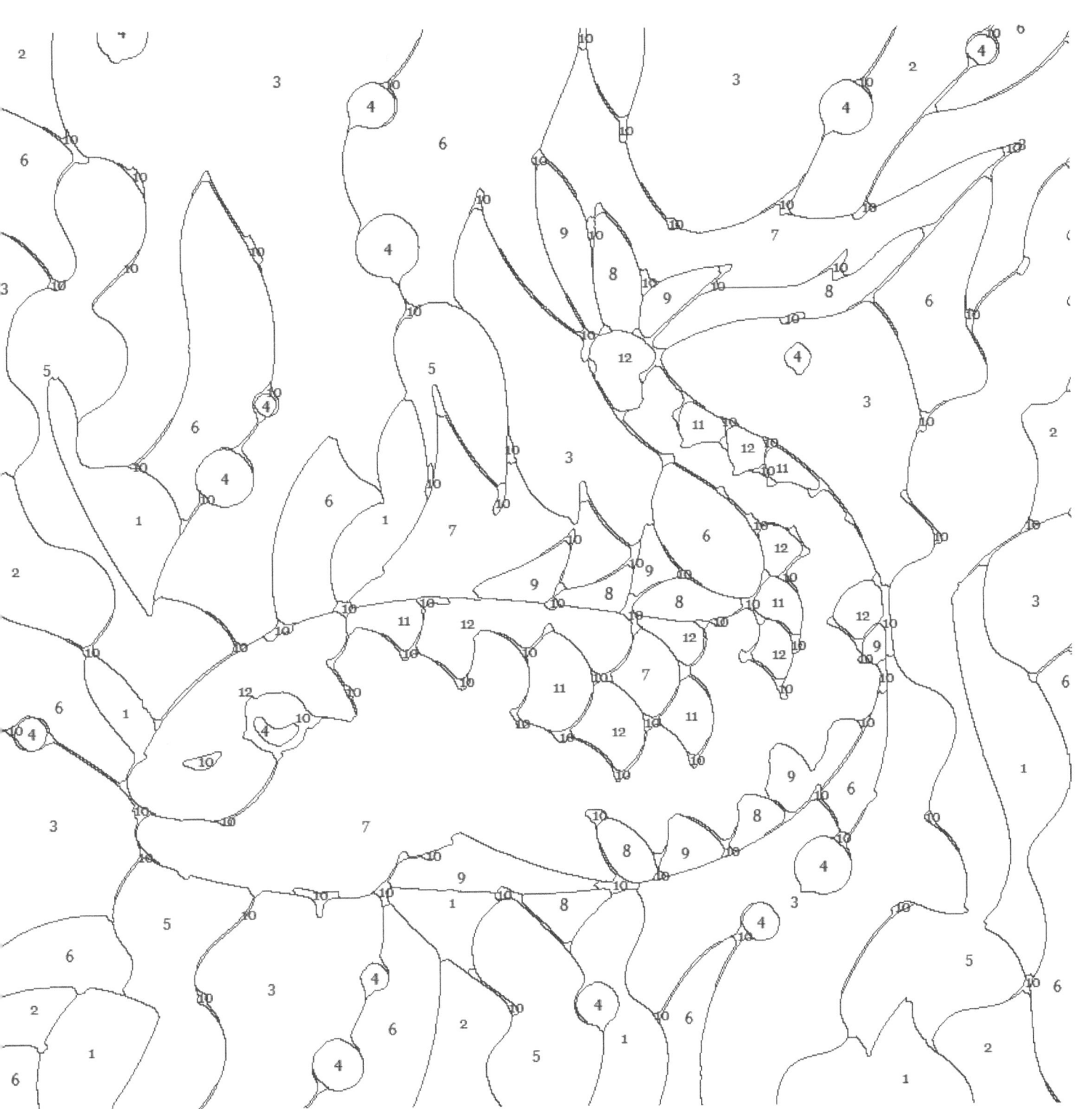

1. Black
2. Blue
3. Light Blue
4. Brown
5. Dark Red
6. Orange
7. Yellow
8. Purple
9. Pink
10. Gold
11. Green
12. Gold
13. Red
14. Dark Green

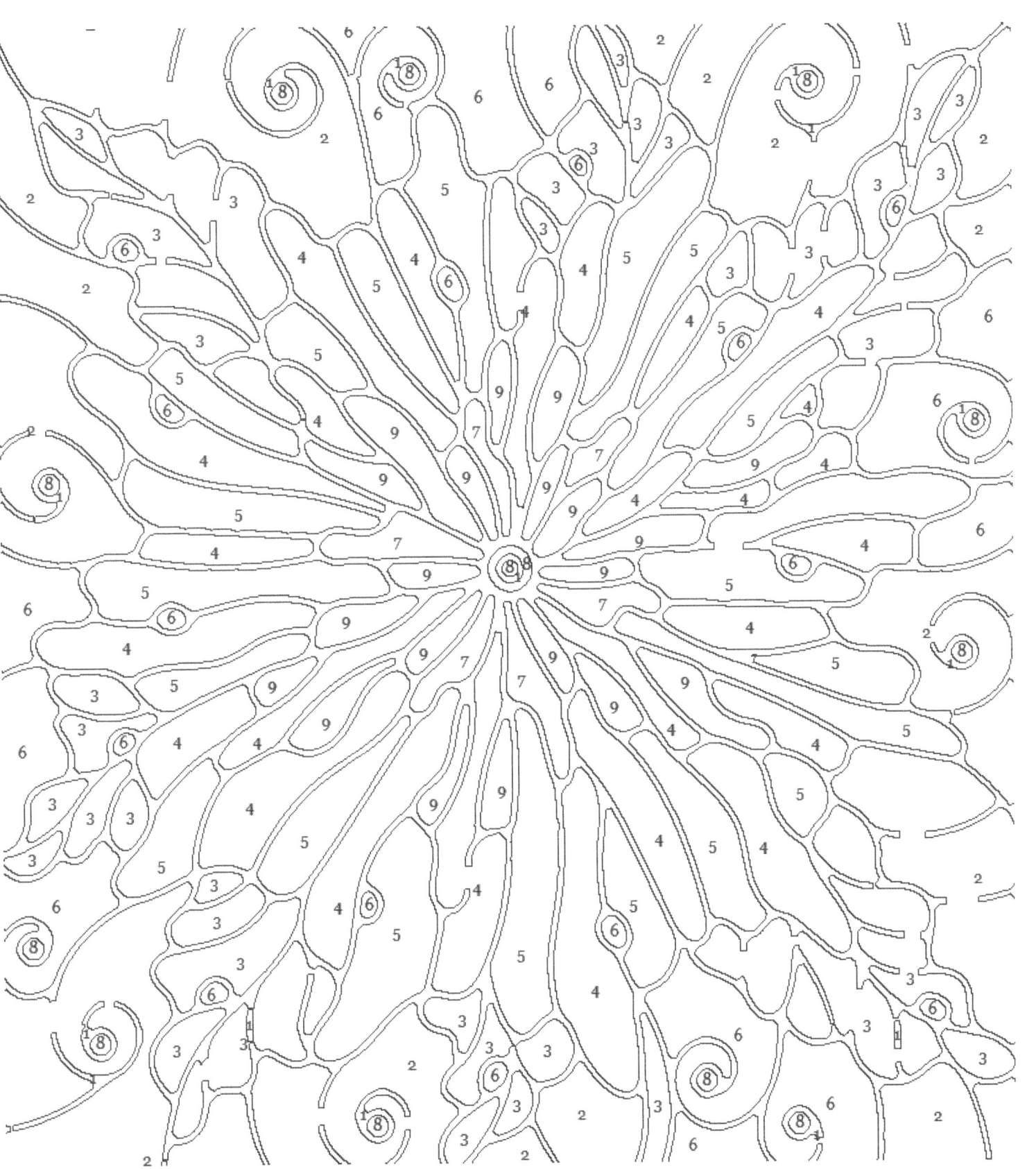

1. Black
2. Blue
3. Light Blue
4. Brown
5. Dark Red
6. Orange
7. Yellow
8. Purple
9. Pink
10. Gold
11. Green
12. Gold
13. Red
14. Dark Green

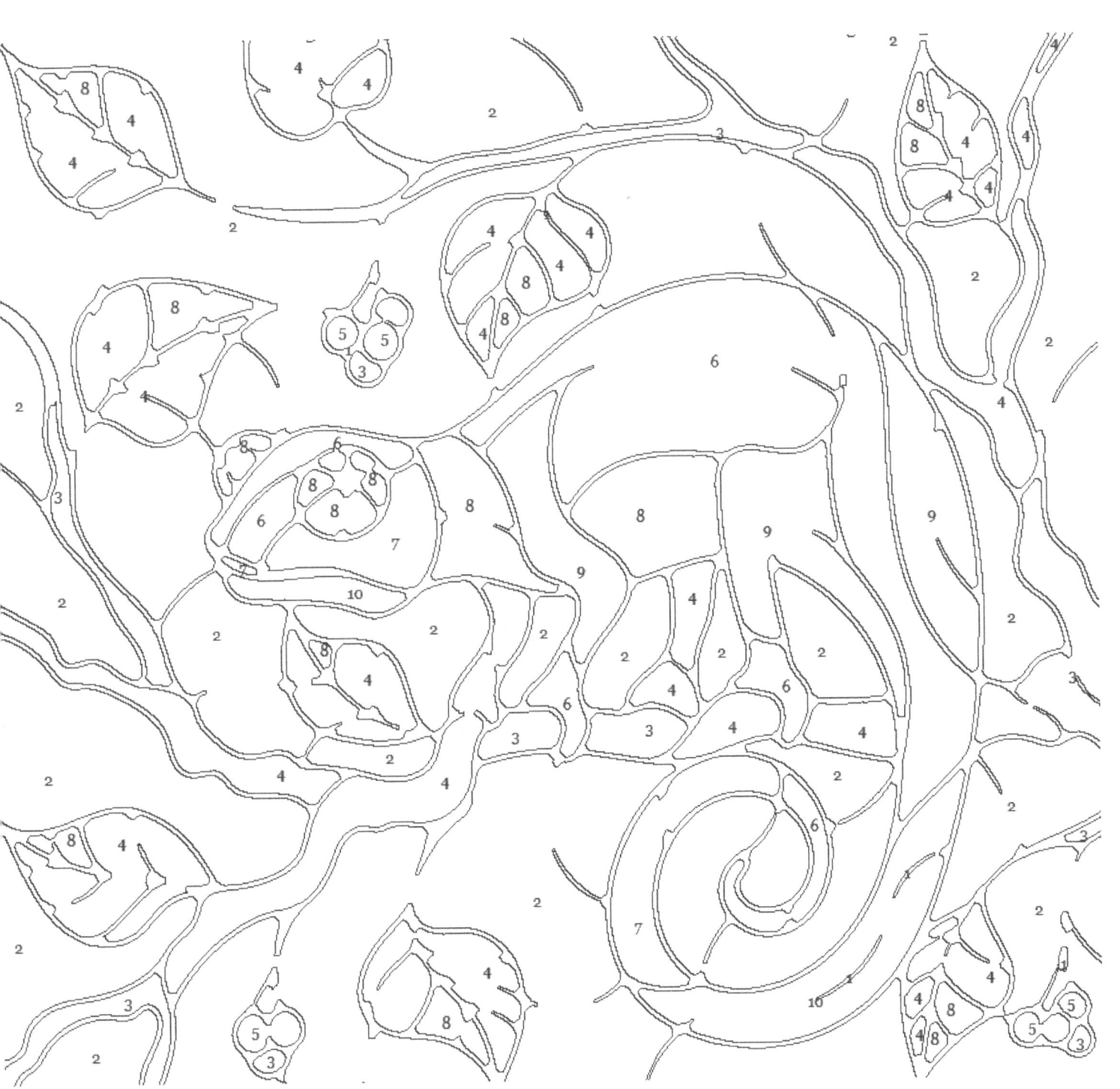

1. Black
2. Blue
3. Light Blue
4. Brown
5. Dark Red
6. Orange
7. Yellow
8. Purple
9. Pink
10. Gold
11. Green
12. Gold
13. Red
14. Dark Green

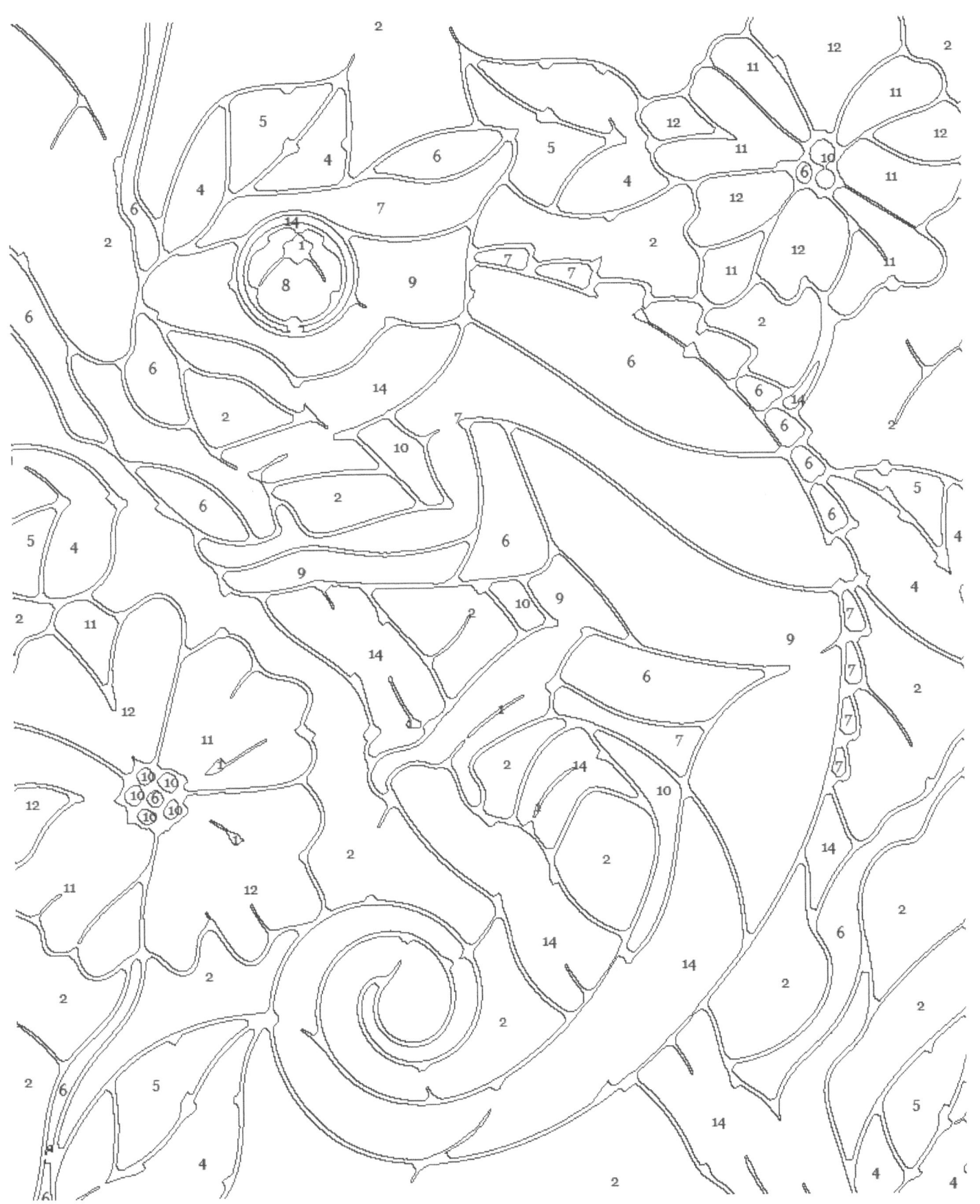

1. Black
2. Blue
3. Light Blue
4. Brown
5. Dark Red
6. Orange
7. Yellow
8. Purple
9. Pink
10. Gold
11. Green
12. Gold
13. Red
14. Dark Green

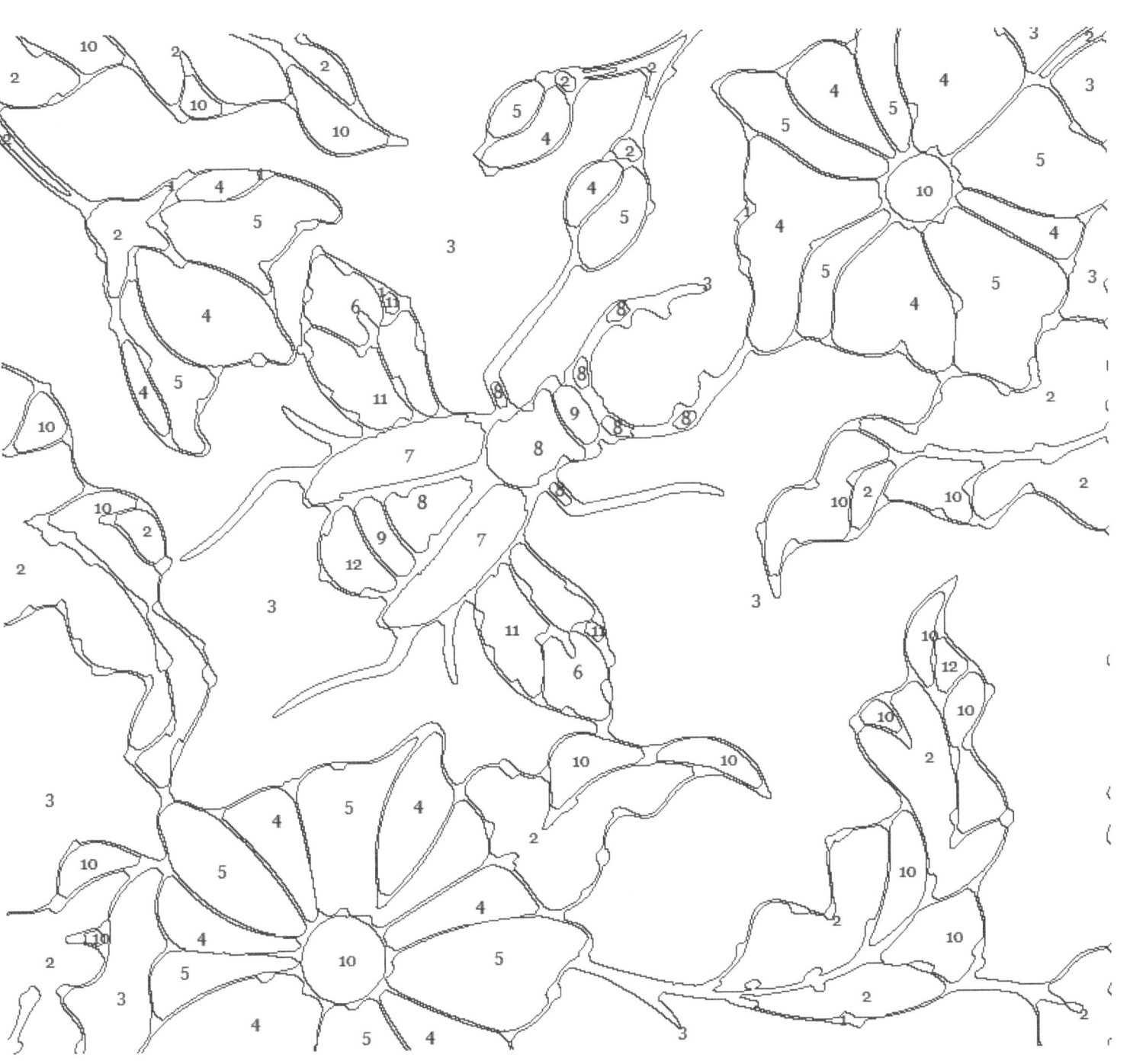

1. Black
2. Blue
3. Light Blue
4. Brown
5. Dark Red
6. Orange
7. Yellow
8. Purple
9. Pink
10. Gold
11. Green
12. Gold
13. Red
14. Dark Green

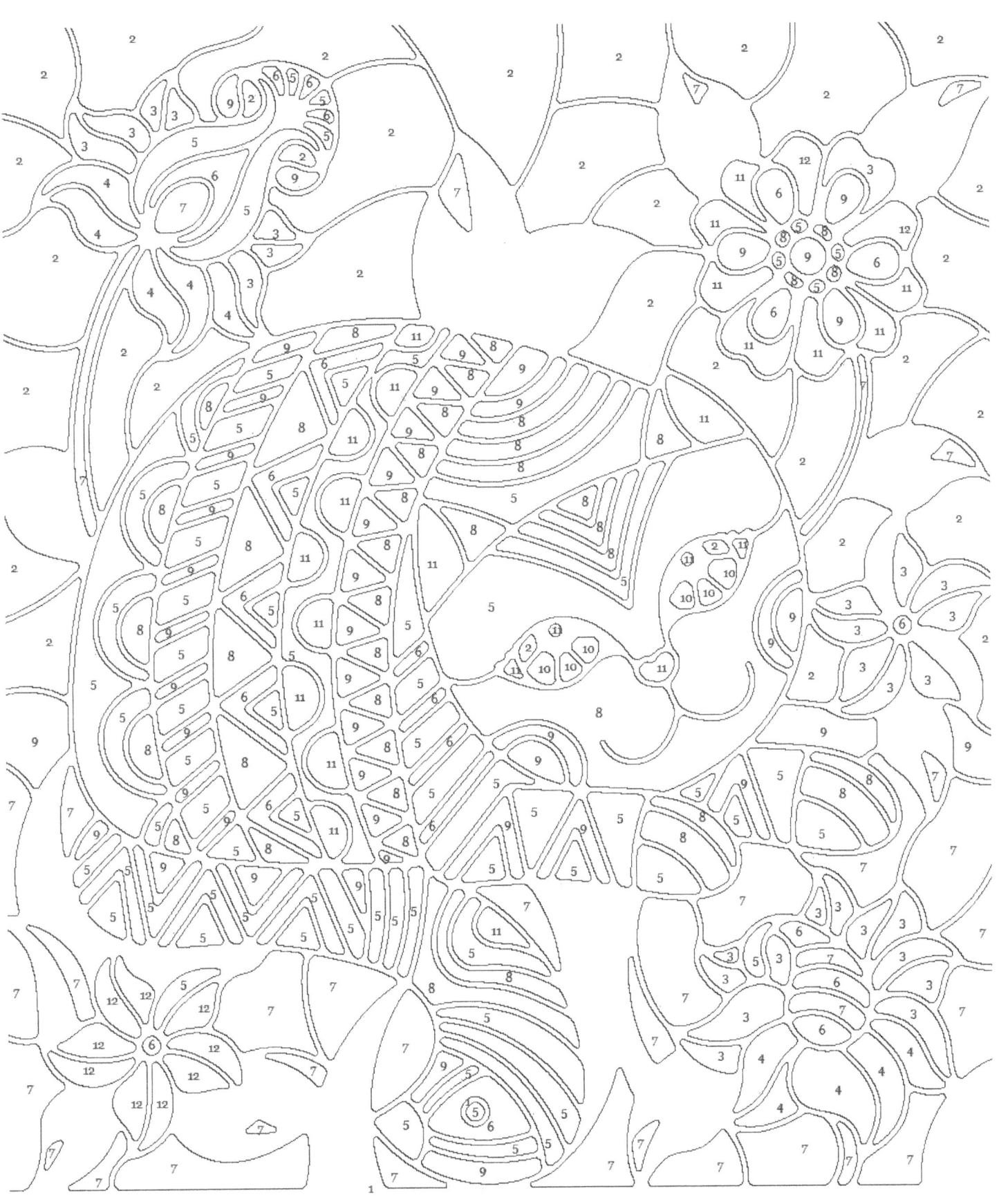

1. Black
2. Blue
3. Light Blue
4. Brown
5. Dark Red
6. Orange
7. Yellow
8. Purple
9. Pink
10. Gold
11. Green
12. Gold
13. Red
14. Dark Green

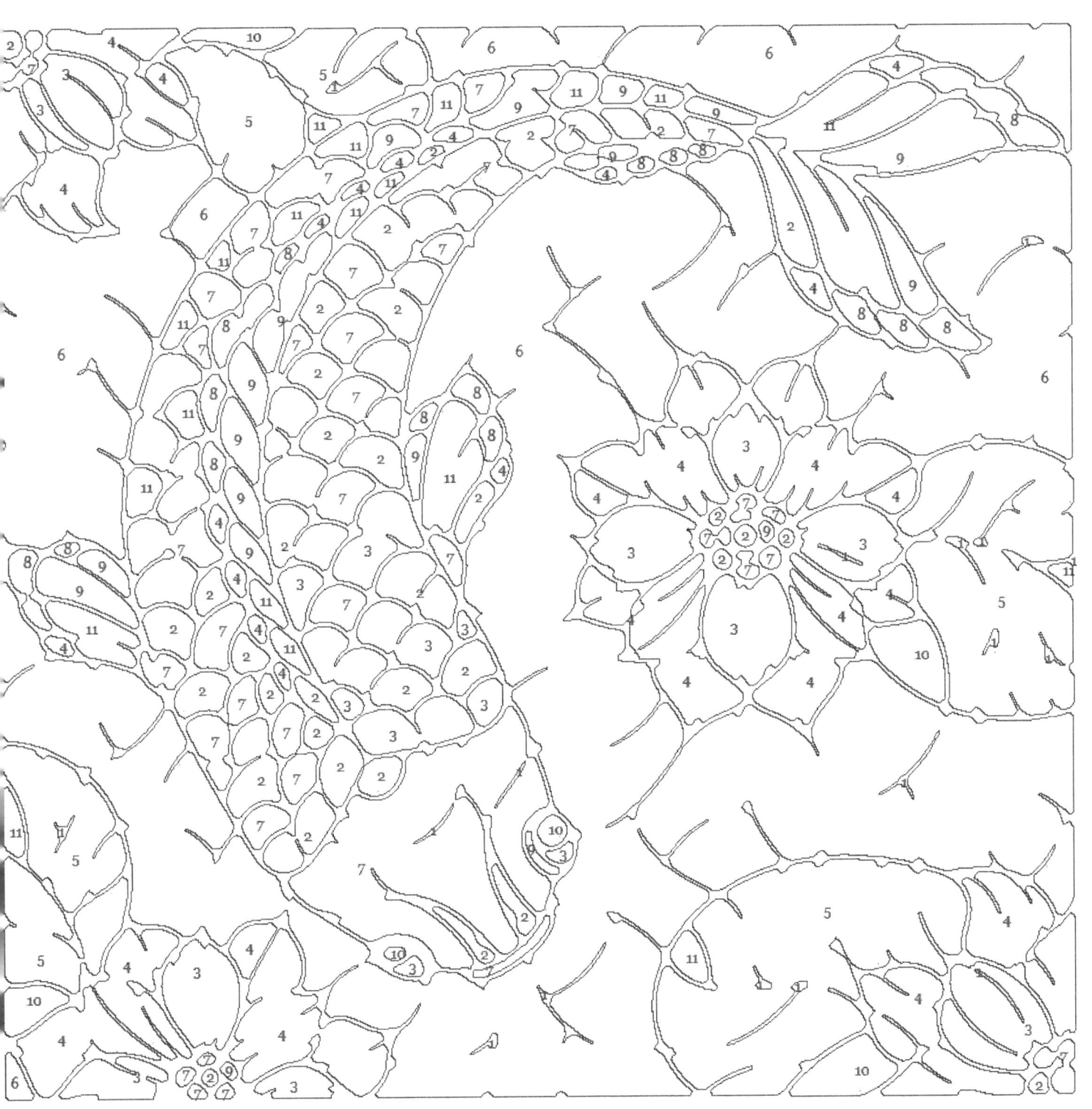

1. Black
2. Blue
3. Light Blue
4. Brown
5. Dark Red
6. Orange
7. Yellow
8. Purple
9. Pink
10. Gold
11. Green
12. Gold
13. Red
14. Dark Green

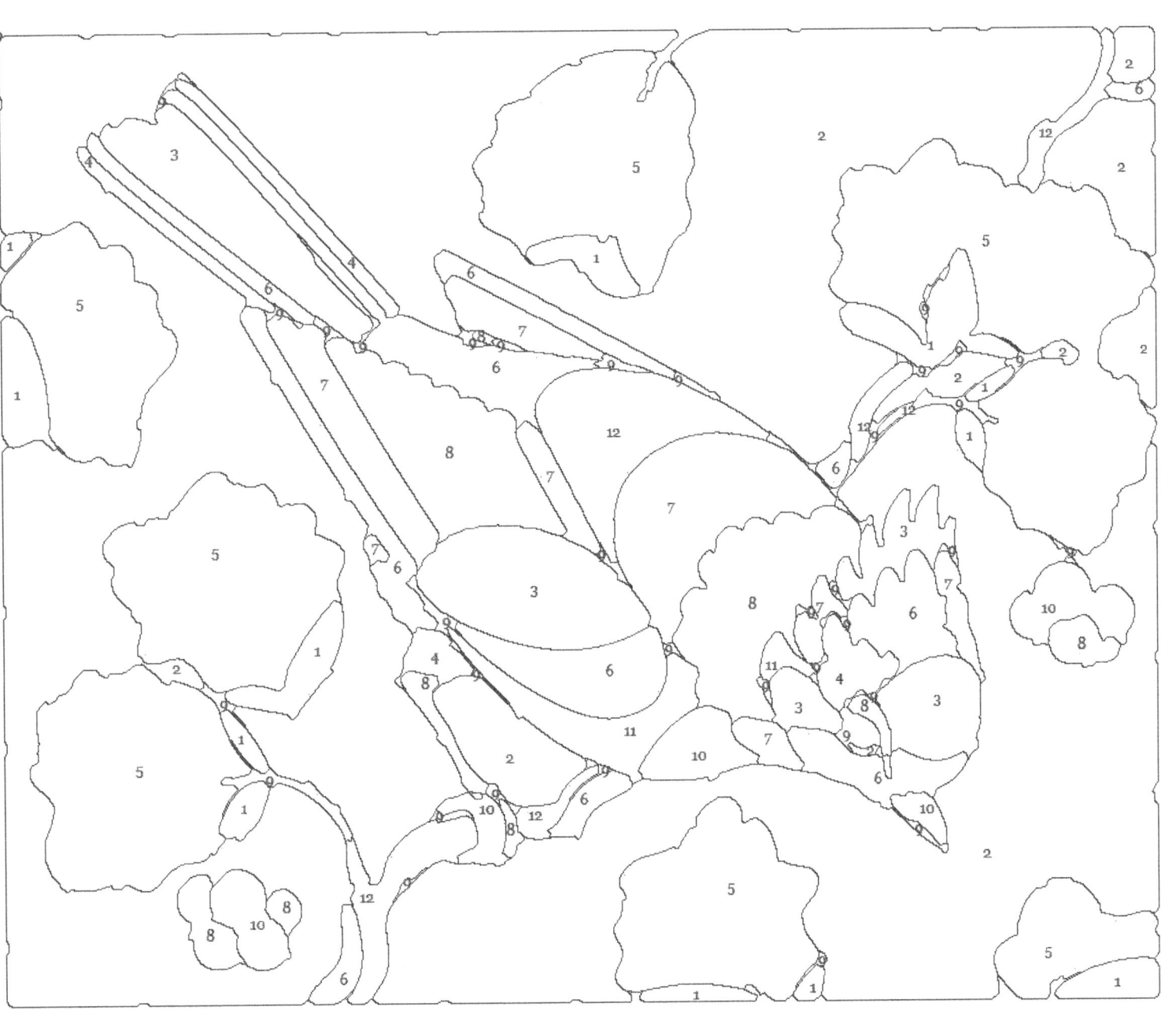

1. Black
2. Blue
3. Light Blue
4. Brown
5. Dark Red
6. Orange
7. Yellow
8. Purple
9. Pink
10. Gold
11. Green
12. Gold
13. Red
14. Dark Green

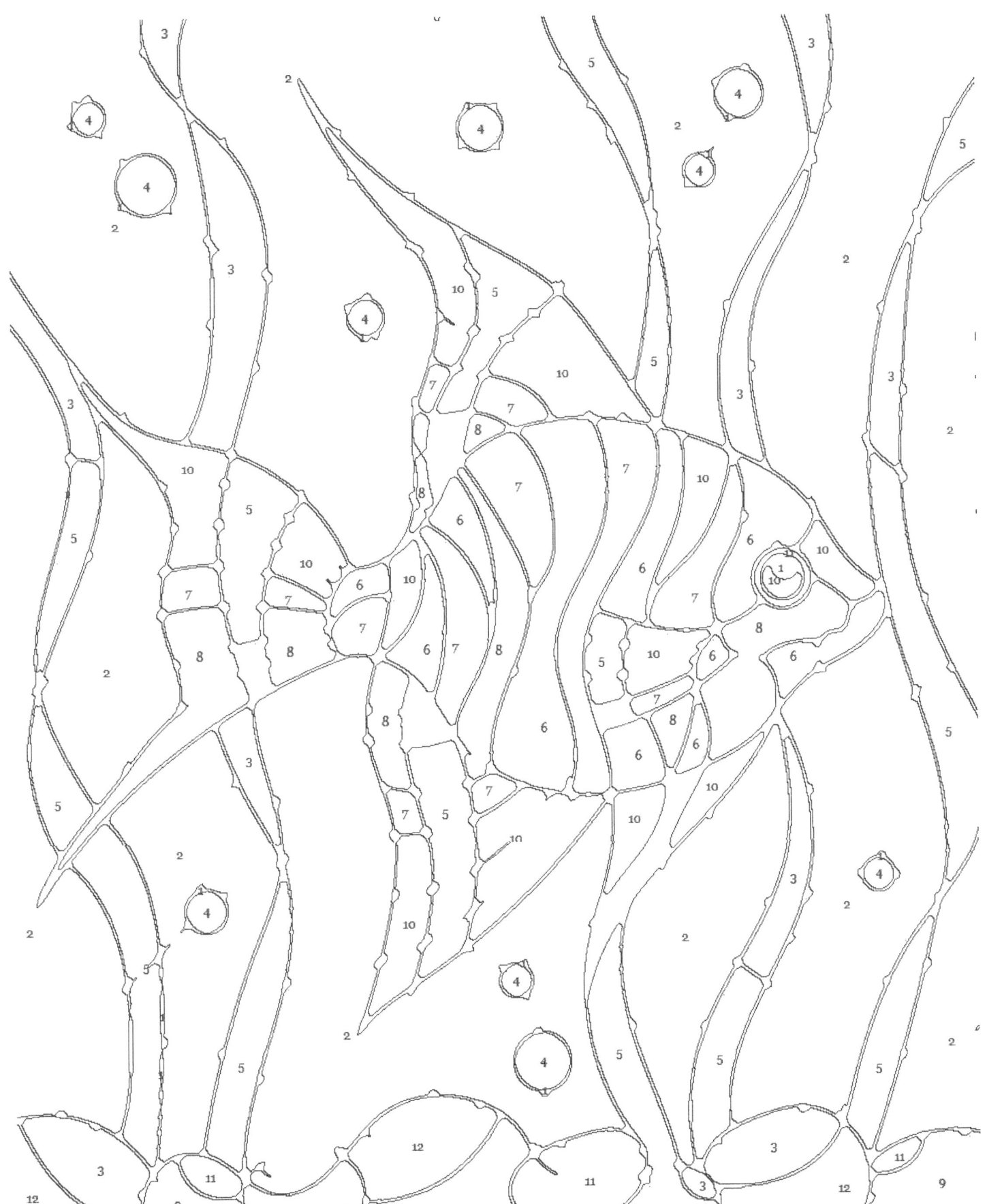

1. Black
2. Blue
3. Light Blue
4. Brown
5. Dark Red
6. Orange
7. Yellow
8. Purple
9. Pink
10. Gold
11. Green
12. Gold
13. Red
14. Dark Green

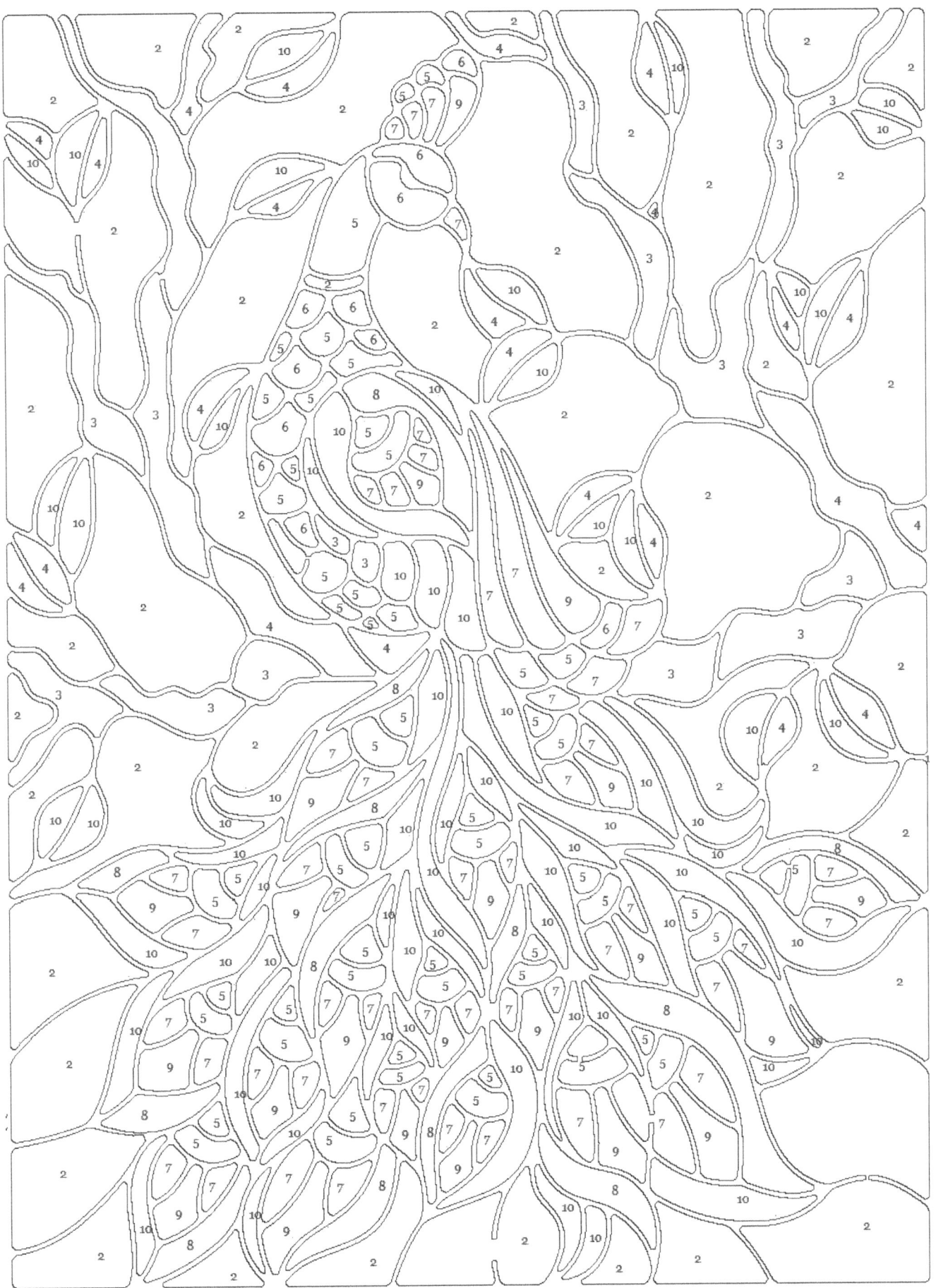

1. Black
2. Blue
3. Light Blue
4. Brown
5. Dark Red
6. Orange
7. Yellow
8. Purple
9. Pink
10. Gold
11. Green
12. Gold
13. Red
14. Dark Green

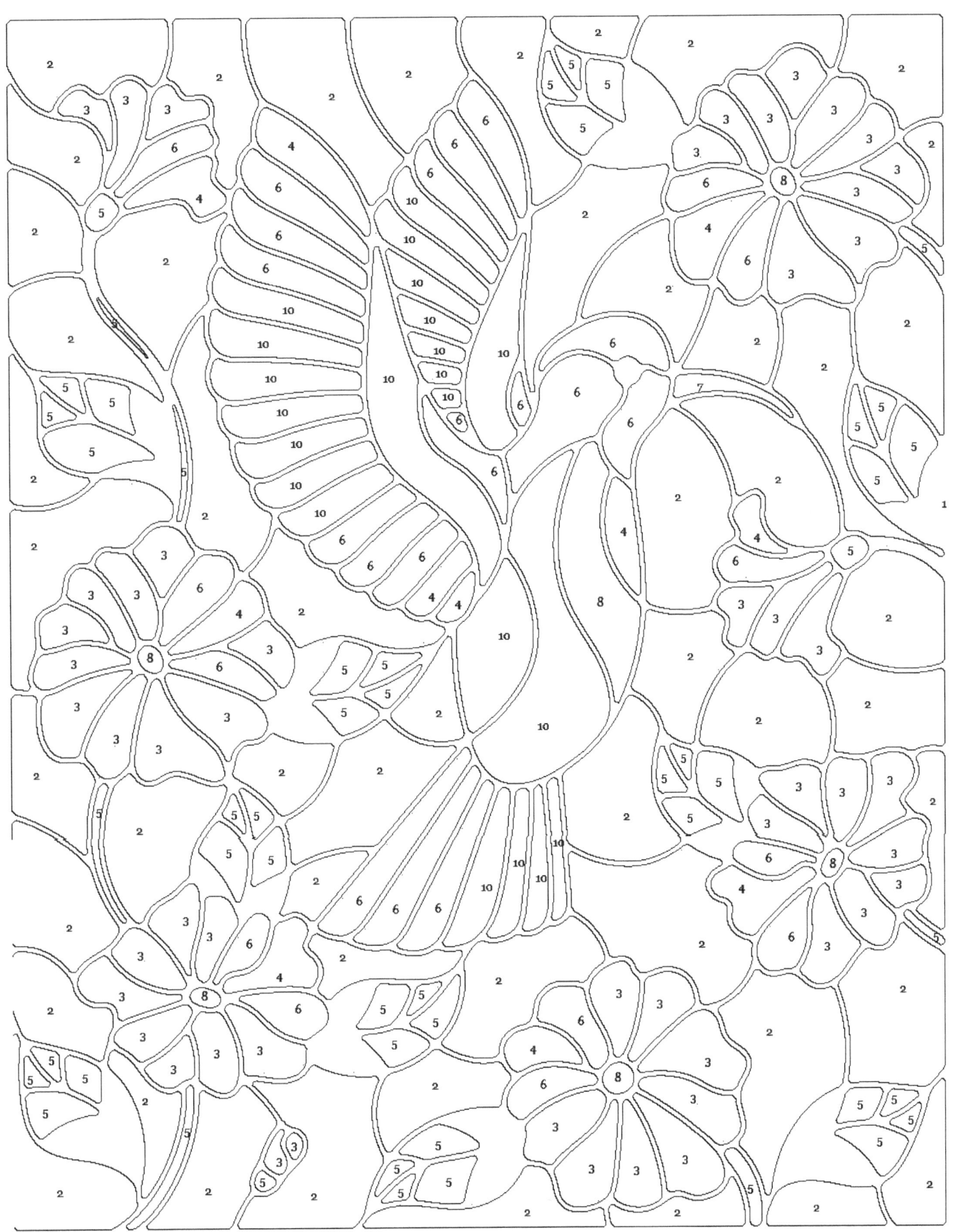

www.ingramcontent.com/pod-product-compliance
Lightning Source LLC
Chambersburg PA
CBHW081103240526
45465CB00026B/3304